3/98

I Heal

I Heal

The Children of Chernobyl in Cuba

*by Trish Marx &
Dorita Beh-Eger
photographs by Cindy Karp*

Lerner Publications Company ■ Minneapolis

Illustration on pp. 6–7 by John Erste. Map on p. 11 by Laura Westlund.

Library of Congress Cataloging-in-Publication Data

Marx, Trish.
   I heal : the children of Chernobyl in Cuba / by Trish Marx and Dorita
Beh-Eger ; photographs by Cindy Karp.
     p.   c.m.
   Summary: A photo essay about young victims of the Chernobyl nuclear
accident who are receiving medical treatment in Cuba.
   ISBN 0-8225-4897-6 (alk. paper)
   1. Tumors in children—Treatment—Ukraine—Pictorial works—Juvenile
literature. 2. Tumors in children—Treatment—Cuba—Pictorial works—
Juvenile literature. 3. Chernobyl Nuclear Accident, Chornobyl´, Ukraine,
1986—Health aspects—Pictorial works—Juvenile literature. 4. Radiation
victims—Medical care—International cooperation—Pictorial works—
Juvenile literature. [1. Tumors—Patients. 2. Chernobyl Nuclear Accident,
Chornobyl´, Ukraine, 1986. 3. Radiation victims.] I. Beh-Eger, Dorita.
II. Karp, Cindy, ill. III. Title.
RC281.C4M365   1996
618.92′9897—dc20   95-53927

To John Otterpohl, for his vision and understanding of the human condition, and, with many thanks, to Ellie Temple and Becka McKay—TM

To Joseph Eger, for his passionate dedication to peace and the welfare of the world's children—DBE

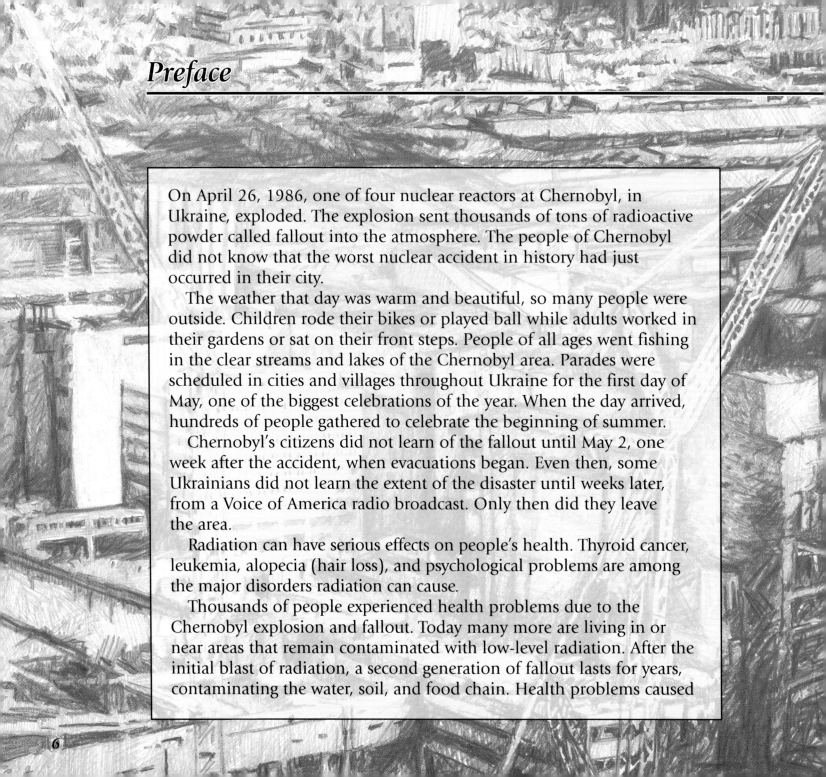

Preface

On April 26, 1986, one of four nuclear reactors at Chernobyl, in Ukraine, exploded. The explosion sent thousands of tons of radioactive powder called fallout into the atmosphere. The people of Chernobyl did not know that the worst nuclear accident in history had just occurred in their city.

The weather that day was warm and beautiful, so many people were outside. Children rode their bikes or played ball while adults worked in their gardens or sat on their front steps. People of all ages went fishing in the clear streams and lakes of the Chernobyl area. Parades were scheduled in cities and villages throughout Ukraine for the first day of May, one of the biggest celebrations of the year. When the day arrived, hundreds of people gathered to celebrate the beginning of summer.

Chernobyl's citizens did not learn of the fallout until May 2, one week after the accident, when evacuations began. Even then, some Ukrainians did not learn the extent of the disaster until weeks later, from a Voice of America radio broadcast. Only then did they leave the area.

Radiation can have serious effects on people's health. Thyroid cancer, leukemia, alopecia (hair loss), and psychological problems are among the major disorders radiation can cause.

Thousands of people experienced health problems due to the Chernobyl explosion and fallout. Today many more are living in or near areas that remain contaminated with low-level radiation. After the initial blast of radiation, a second generation of fallout lasts for years, contaminating the water, soil, and food chain. Health problems caused

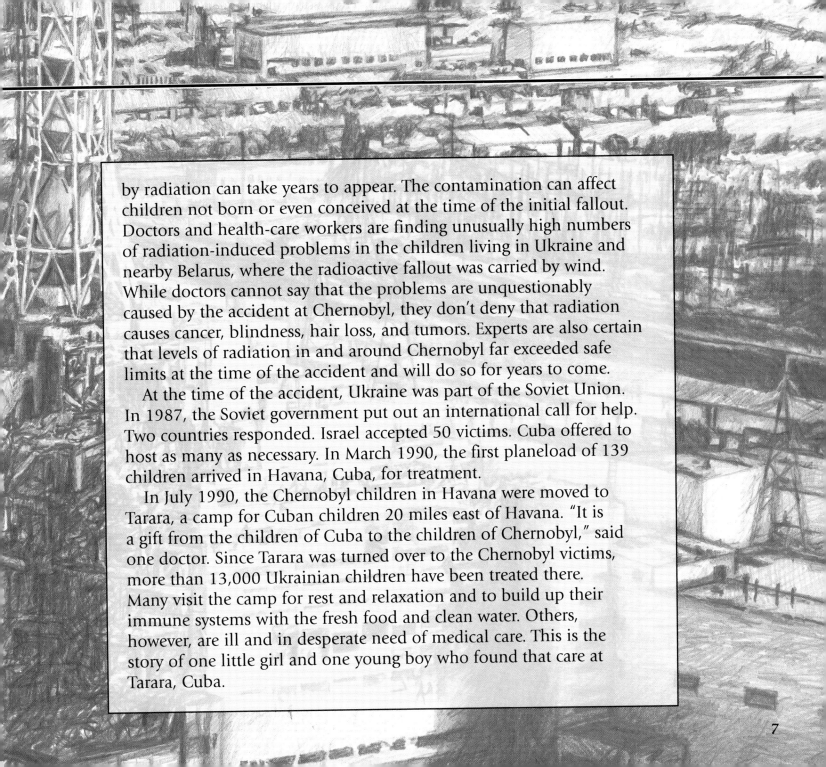

by radiation can take years to appear. The contamination can affect children not born or even conceived at the time of the initial fallout. Doctors and health-care workers are finding unusually high numbers of radiation-induced problems in the children living in Ukraine and nearby Belarus, where the radioactive fallout was carried by wind. While doctors cannot say that the problems are unquestionably caused by the accident at Chernobyl, they don't deny that radiation causes cancer, blindness, hair loss, and tumors. Experts are also certain that levels of radiation in and around Chernobyl far exceeded safe limits at the time of the accident and will do so for years to come.

At the time of the accident, Ukraine was part of the Soviet Union. In 1987, the Soviet government put out an international call for help. Two countries responded. Israel accepted 50 victims. Cuba offered to host as many as necessary. In March 1990, the first planeload of 139 children arrived in Havana, Cuba, for treatment.

In July 1990, the Chernobyl children in Havana were moved to Tarara, a camp for Cuban children 20 miles east of Havana. "It is a gift from the children of Cuba to the children of Chernobyl," said one doctor. Since Tarara was turned over to the Chernobyl victims, more than 13,000 Ukrainian children have been treated there. Many visit the camp for rest and relaxation and to build up their immune systems with the fresh food and clean water. Others, however, are ill and in desperate need of medical care. This is the story of one little girl and one young boy who found that care at Tarara, Cuba.

My name is Elena Balushko. I was born 12 years ago in Kiev, the capital of Ukraine. The first few years of my life were normal and happy. But when I was two, a nuclear reactor exploded at Chernobyl, sending radiation for miles

around. Much of the radiation reached Kiev. It changed my life forever.

I was very young when the accident occurred, so I know only what my mother has told me. The date was April 26. Everyone was getting excited about the May Day parade. The weather was beautiful.

My parents heard rumors about an explosion, but they did not believe them until a friend, a professor of physics in Kiev, told them to take me away. We left at night so as not to panic the neighbors, and we went to my grandmother's house in Moldova. My parents left me there. When they returned to Kiev a few days later, they learned that the rumors were true.

In the fall I moved back to Kiev for school. I studied ballet and karate. Every summer I would go back to my grandma's house in Moldova, far away from Kiev. The radiation was not as bad there, but people still worried about contamination in the soil, in the water, and in the food we ate.

I got sick when I was nine years old. My nose kept running and bleeding. My mother noticed a lump by my eye. The doctors in Kiev found a tumor growing behind my eye. They operated on it, but it kept getting bigger. My mother took me to another doctor, who said I needed another operation right away. But there was not a bed open in the hospital. The tumor was so big that it changed the shape of my face. I was embarrassed to walk on the street. It affected my balance so that I could not dance or practice karate.

My mother told me later that she wrote to both the Swiss and French governments asking if they could help me. They both told her to take me to Cuba. The Cuban doctors could help me. So my mother quit her job as an electrical engineer. On a plane filled with other Ukrainian children and their mothers, we flew to Cuba.

Not everyone who comes to Tarara needs an operation. Some stay a few months to rest, play in the sun, and eat fresh food. Others stay here a long time. We make friends quickly at Tarara, but I don't have a best friend. All the children are my friends.

The Chernobyl children live in the seaside town of Tarara, where they can play on the beach while they recuperate.

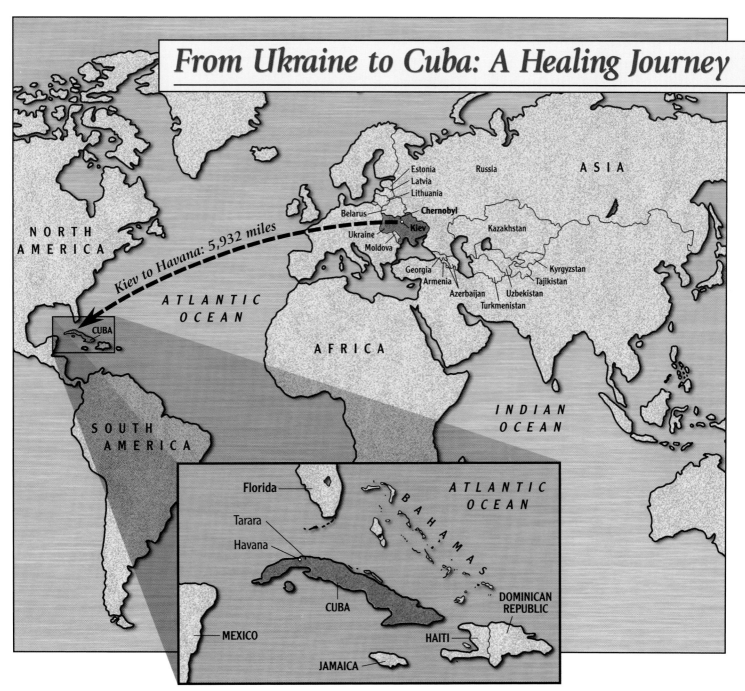

From Ukraine to Cuba: A Healing Journey

Kiev to Havana: 5,932 miles

NORTH AMERICA

SOUTH AMERICA

ATLANTIC OCEAN

AFRICA

ASIA

INDIAN OCEAN

Estonia
Latvia
Lithuania
Belarus
Russia
Chernobyl
Kiev
Ukraine
Moldova
Kazakhstan
Georgia
Armenia
Azerbaijan
Turkmenistan
Uzbekistan
Tajikistan
Kyrgyzstan

CUBA

Florida
Tarara
Havana
CUBA
MEXICO
BAHAMAS
ATLANTIC OCEAN
DOMINICAN REPUBLIC
HAITI
JAMAICA

The first thing I noticed about Tarara was the breeze. It smelled a little salty and a little fishy. Dr. Aurora Freijanes said the smell was from the seaweed in the ocean. I had never been in an ocean, but after I got out of the hospital, I could walk to the beach with my friends. We swim in the early morning or the late afternoon, when the sun is not so strong.

We shared our *casita* (little house) with another mother and her daughter, three other children, and a nurse. We kept all the windows and the front door open and let the sounds and smells of the ocean come in. We decorated the walls with pictures we drew.

Elena and a friend enjoy the warm sun and chase fish in the clear water.

Every day I was taken to a clinic for examinations. I spent most of my first year in Cuba in the hospital in Havana. First I had a biopsy to find out what kind of tumor I had. Then I had chemotherapy, which means I had to take very, very strong medicine to shrink the tumor. Finally, the doctors decided that the whole tumor had to be removed. It covered one side of my face.

This girl (above) is upset to learn that she is not well enough to go home yet.

Treatment often makes the children very tired.

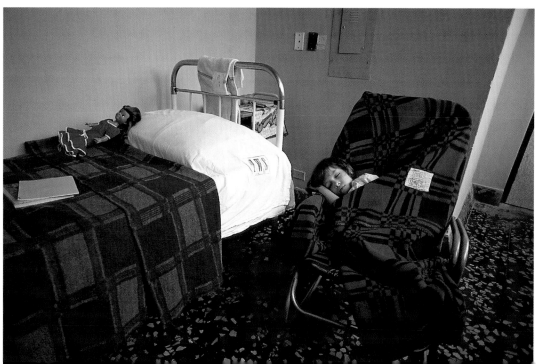

14

Those months in the hospital were difficult and painful. I had to stay there all day for treatments. I couldn't go outdoors because being in the sun made my nose bleed. I missed seeing my friends and going to the beach. But the worst thing was how scared I was. All those treatments! Would they be able to get rid of the tumor? Would my hair ever grow back? Would my face ever look normal again? I was so tired of people staring and pointing and asking questions.

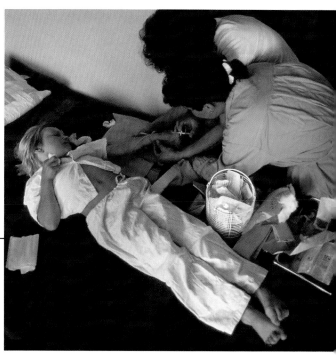

Chemotherapy treatment

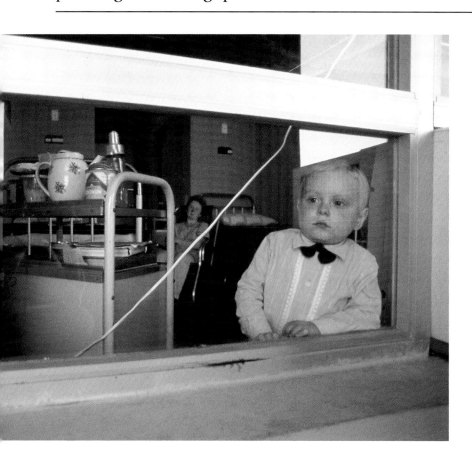

The operation took 10 hours. Twenty doctors were called in to help. When it was over, the tumor was gone. The tumor was very close to my brain, but the doctors said it was not malignant—it did not have cancer cells. The doctors made sure that my hair would cover up the scar.

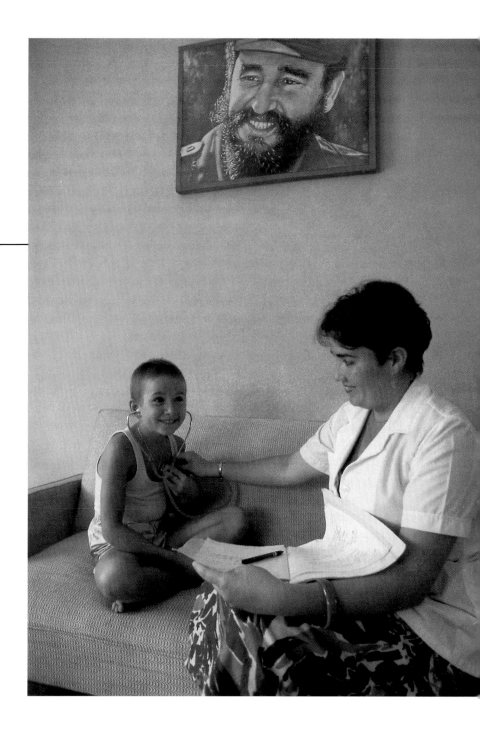

A Cuban doctor does a morning checkup on a young patient.

Dr. Aurora Freijanes (center) *is one of Elena's doctors at Tarara.*

All the doctors and nurses have been extremely kind and helpful. They are very loving. When I had to spend my birthday, January 23, in the hospital, they made a big celebration for me with a huge cake. Parties in the hospital are rare, so this was a special time for me. I felt like a queen! We all played and sang songs for hours until it got dark. We forgot about being sick for a while.

Although some people here speak both Russian and Spanish, it is easier if everyone speaks Spanish. We children are learning faster than our mothers. I learned a lot of Spanish while I was in the hospital in Havana. I had a television in my room, and my mama and I would watch it in the evenings, especially the *novellas* (soap operas). At Tarara the kids are always translating the novellas for their mothers. Some evenings after dinner we watch movies. A few nights ago we saw *War and Peace.*

I love to read, especially books about nature, animals, and flowers. I just finished reading a book about the migration of birds. I've also read two plays by William Shakespeare: *Romeo and Juliet* and *King Lear*. There is even a small theater where we perform plays and shows with music and dancing.

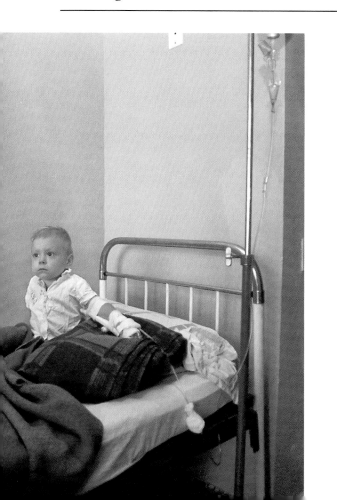

Elena spends a lot of time reading—by herself and with friends. Center: *A mother reads to her child in the hospital.*

Of course, dancing is what I enjoy most. I'm learning the Cuban dances. We sing the *macarena*—a popular new song—while doing the steps over and over. My friends and I perform it for visitors and for festivals. We learn other dances, too, and many of the songs and poems of Cuba. In Ukraine, I never knew about salsa dancing. It's a fun, fast kind of dancing that we love. We don't even wait for a party. We just put the music on and dance!

Playing games and spending time together helps distract the children from the difficulties of their illnesses. Chess (opposite) *is especially popular.*

One of the houses has a room where we can play on computers. We play war games, number games, and racing games. That room is always noisy, and it's just for kids. None of the doctors can play the games as well as we can.

Once a week we go on trips into Havana. Sometimes we go to a museum or to the aquarium. We are learning about Cuban history and life. *Habana Vieja*, the old city, has narrow cobblestone streets, and all the buildings look as they did hundreds of years ago. We visit the art galleries there and also the outdoor exhibits of work by local artisans. The people we meet sometimes know we are from Chernobyl and are very

Elena and her friend Lubomir (above) *chat with the street vendors of* **Habana Vieja** *(Old Havana).*

cheerful and kind to us. One day a man selling straw hats in the plaza (town square) smiled at us and asked, "You like my hats?" When we asked him how much his hats cost, he said, "Are you the Chernobyl children? You can have these hats as a gift." We all returned home that day wearing big handmade sombreros.

We all feel safe and protected here in this village. We can walk freely, ride bikes, and play without worrying about our safety. The teachers, the coaches, and the cooks are all our good friends.

When some children were very homesick, they wouldn't eat. I felt that way at first. I preferred to have breakfast in our casita instead of in the cafeteria with most of the other children. So the cooks and our mothers would sometimes make us a special Ukrainian breakfast of ham, fried eggs, *sirniki* (cheese pancakes), and potato pancakes. Cuban breakfasts are usually fruit—such as mangoes or bananas—and dry toast. Now I have come to like the food here, especially mangoes!

Elena and her mother rely on each other. For a special treat, Elena's mother made a cake out of pancakes!

Just before my big operation, the one that removed all of the tumor, a friend of mine died. I had been in the hospital in Cuba for one year, and my friend and I had made each other cards and painted pictures to help distract us from our treatments. No one told me about his death until after my operation—not the nurses, not my mother, not the other children. They did not want me to be afraid.

Sometimes the surgeon in charge of my operation would take me to her house so that my mother could have a chance to rest. The surgeon would cook me special food and take good care of me. Some of the children in the hospital had to stay in bed all the time. One little girl could not walk around, and on the weekends when I left the hospital I tried to take her a flower or something pretty to cheer her up. The nurses also played with us or read us books when they were not giving treatments.

Resting during hospital treatment

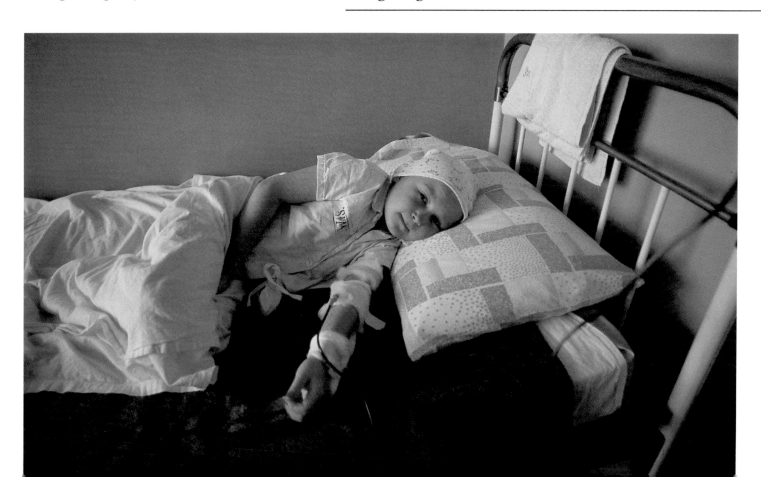

Many of the children have no hair when they come to Cuba. Others lose their hair from cancer treatments.

Some children are bald when they come here. They have lost their hair from living with low levels of radiation. The Cubans have a special lotion that they put on the scalps of these children, and often the hair grows back. I lost my hair when I had chemotherapy, but it grew back. None of us seem to mind losing our hair because so many of us are all the same, with no hair. Other children have vitiligo—large blotches of discolored skin—which might be caused by radiation, too.

Having a parent or grandparent in Cuba eases some of the loneliness and fear.

All the children are checked for their level of radiation when they first arrive. Perhaps the most common illness here has to do with the thyroid gland, which is very sensitive to radiation. Many other children have leukemia, a disease of the blood. And still other children have tumors, as I did. My mother thought she was alone with my problem until she came here. Then she saw how many children from our country need treatment.

Some children are here because the doctors in Ukraine want them to spend time in the warm weather—swimming and playing, eating fresh fruit and drinking uncontaminated milk—away from the worry of living in Ukraine. They stay about a month and a half and go home looking healthy.

The doctors from Tarara and the Ukrainian doctors they work with cannot send all of the sick children to Cuba. Treatment is very expensive, and often the drugs are not available. But we are all very important to the Cuban doctors. They come to Tarara, sometimes without breakfast, traveling on their bicycles or by bus from Havana and not leaving Tarara until long after dark.

Dr. Freijanes gives daily medicine to a reluctant patient.

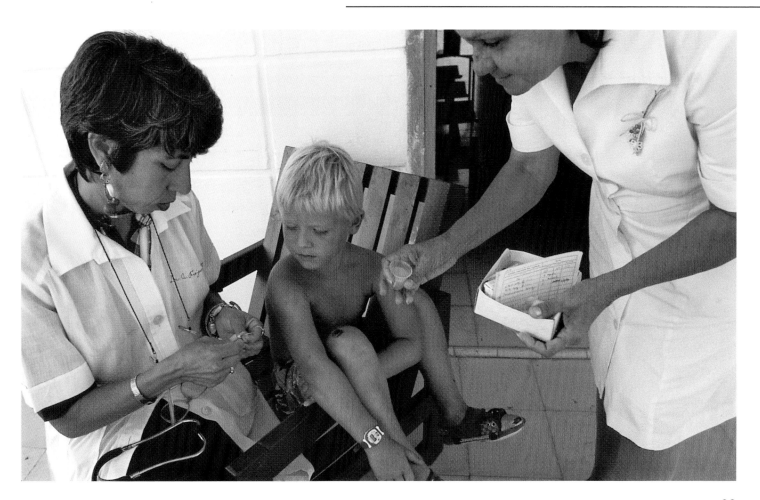

My friend Lubo has been here almost as long as I have. He had a tumor on his neck. He told me the story of when he found out he needed an operation:

Lubo could understand all the Spanish words the doctors were saying. They were asking his mother's permission for his operation. "I want to assure you," one doctor said to her, "that your son is going to live if we can remove the remaining tumor."

Lubo interrupted them. He jumped up and cried out, "If this operation will help me, I want to have it. I want to live."

His name is Lubomir Gslinskaya, but everyone calls him Lubo. He's 11 years old, and he came here from a village in Ukraine called Sterno-pylskaya, where he lived with his parents and his older brother.

At the time of the accident in Chernobyl, Lubo was only a year old. Like me, he doesn't remember anything about it, only what his parents have told him.

When he was three, he started getting colds and coughs and fevers all the time. One day his mother noticed a small lump on his neck. When a doctor examined the lump, he said it was just a swollen gland and told Lubo's mother to put hot compresses on *it. But it kept growing and growing. The doctors suggested that Lubo go to a doctor who knew about tumors.*

His parents took him to a hospital in a nearby town. Tests showed that Lubo had cancer. He had to stay in the hospital a very long time...six months! He remembers being very scared. He didn't understand what was happening to him. He felt sick all the time from the strong medicines the doctors gave him. At least his mother was allowed to stay with him in his hospital room.

After a few months, the tumor on his neck started to shrink little by little. He began to feel better and could go home to be with his family again. But two years later, the illness returned. The lump grew back, much bigger than before—like a grapefruit. Lubo was terrified.

Lubo's mother heard about some doctors who had come to Ukraine from Cuba. These doctors knew a lot about illnesses from radiation. When his mother took him to one of those doctors, she started to cry. The doctor told her, "Don't cry. Everything will be fine. We will take care of your son the best way we know." As soon as they could, Lubo and his mother came to Tarara.

31

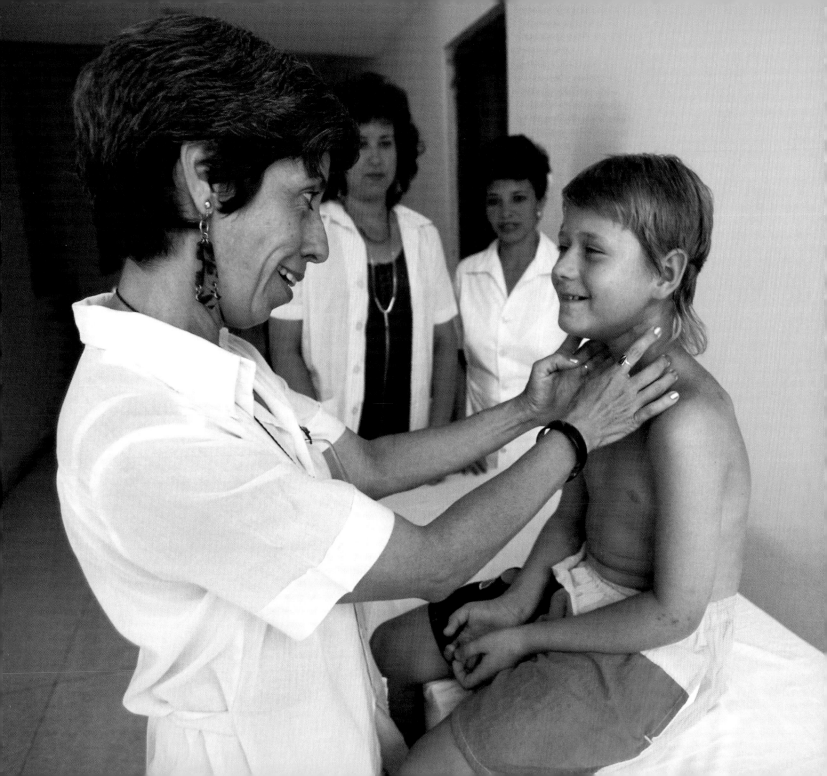

Lubo and his mother

When Lubo came to Cuba, he received chemotherapy treatments every day to reduce the size of his tumor. After a few months, the tumor shrank. The little bit that remained needed to be removed by surgery, so Lubo had an operation. Now, after many months, he is free of this cancer. He feels good and acts like any normal boy.

When Lubo had to be in the hospital on his birthday, March 28, the doctors and nurses all made a little party for him, just like they did for me. When he returned to Tarara, we had another party for him.

The kids here are great. We get along well because we have many of the same physical problems and we understand how difficult and frightening they can be. When Lubo had his operation, we sent him funny drawings to make him laugh. One of the boys lent him his tape player so he could listen to music during his treatments. Lubo especially likes Michael Jackson.

Lubo and Elena make a new friend.

Lubo loves to play chess.

Lubo is getting healthier and stronger every day. He doesn't miss very much about his life in Ukraine. Here at Tarara, he's learned to do karate and to play baseball. Lubo's good at computer games, too. He tells us he used to ride a pony and would love to do that again someday. He rides his bike everywhere around our little village. He has a close friend in Ukraine—Mischa, whom he sometimes misses—but in Tarara he's made new friends: Sergei, Stas, and Andrei. They all play chess with him just like Mischa did at home in Ukraine.

Lubo and I—and all of our friends—love going to the beach more than anything. We like swimming in the ocean or just floating on the salty water and looking up at the clouds drifting above. From our casita, there is a long pathway with trees and shrubs winding down to the beach and the bright blue ocean. In Ukraine we have only a lake for swimming—it can be very cold! Here we can play in the warm sand, the sunshine, and the clean, fresh air.

Lubo practices his underwater handstands. In Habana Vieja (opposite), *he finds some old cannons to jump on.*

Lubo likes the food here, too, especially bananas, pineapple, and grapes. His mama says he's becoming more Cuban than Ukrainian. She laughs and says, "He's such a good boy, but he's bad, bad, bad!" She probably means he's too rowdy sometimes and doesn't always do what she'd like. We think Lubo is fun.

No one knows exactly how much longer Lubo will stay at Tarara. The doctors want to be sure he is completely well, so he may stay a few months longer for treatment and examinations. He will also keep on studying, playing baseball, and going to the beach. When it's time to return to his country, he says, he'll go back to school and be a great baseball player and make all the calls in Spanish.

Some children come to Tarara and never seem to leave. Christina came to Tarara when it first opened because she was born without hipbones. She has had 10 operations and needs one more. Although she is tiny, she sings more loudly than anyone else, and she walks—and runs—all over. Our festival days would not be the same without Christina singing at the microphone and her mother playing the piano for all of us.

The plants and flowers of tropical Cuba are very different from plants found in Ukraine.

40

Although everyone comes to Tarara sick and afraid, they soon learn that it is a healing place. Living in Cuba is difficult because the Cubans suffer from shortages of food and medicine. But the Cubans give us everything that we need. When people come and visit, they always ask what we do all day. My friend Ulua says that is a silly question. She always answers, "I heal."

If I had stayed in Ukraine, maybe I would be fine today. Maybe a space in the hospital would have been found, maybe doctors there would have removed the tumor, maybe I would be back in my old school. But my mama says that here in Tarara more than my tumor has been healed. She says that here in Tarara my spirit has been healed, too.

Elena misses her cat, Snowy, who is home in Ukraine.

42

Afterword

The children who come to Tarara are chosen by their doctors in Ukraine. Once they arrive, they are given a medical examination and put into one of four categories by their Cuban doctors, with help from their records from home. The first category includes children who are very sick with leukemia and tumors; the second category includes children who are believed to be ill and need observation and tests; the third category includes children with skin diseases such as alopecia and vitiligo. Children in

45

the fourth category are not necessarily ill but are in Cuba for the chance to live in an environment free of radiation and to build up their immune systems. All of these children come from contaminated areas in Ukraine. The seriously ill children are treated in Havana hospitals; the rest are treated at the clinic in Tarara.

The children are guaranteed proper nutrition, a healing environment, and recreational and cultural activities, as well as medical care. When they are feeling well enough, they attend classes to help them keep up with their classmates in Ukraine.

Although Cuba is a small country, an island in the Caribbean isolated from large medical centers, it is well known for its excellent medical facilities. The United States, however, has for many years imposed an embargo, or boycott, against Cuba because the two countries disagree on how Cuba should be governed. Partly because of the embargo and partly because of the collapse of the Soviet Union— whose government once provided many goods to the Cubans— medical supplies, gasoline, and even food are very scarce. What the Cubans do have, they share with the children of Chernobyl. Many more children could be treated, however, if more money and resources were available.

Acknowledgments

Thanks to the following people and organizations for their help and support:

Maryann and Allison MacDonald; the Cuban Mission of the United Nations, New York City; Olga Teresa Perez Berra; Alicia Perea; Dorita Luisa Beh; the doctors and staff at Tarara; Michael Tacheny; Ada Wasserman; Dr. Marina Ostanniy; Molly Marx; Dr. Michelle Rossman; and Dr. Ralph Dale and Hendrina Ophey.

Trish Marx and Dorita Beh-Eger

My husband, J. M. Burgos, for his relentless support; Dr. Ernesto and Estela Bravo; Dr. Aurora Freijanes; and Black Star Photo Agency, New York.

Cindy Karp